In Memoriam
Presented to

Dennis Stratton
Cremin Memorial
Learning Center

by

Mr. & Mrs. Melville Knirsch
In Memory of

John S. Steffens

Tony Chen

Some animals in the *Day in the Woods* hunt for food
in the morning or late afternoon.

A Day in the Woods

By Ronald M. Fisher
Photographs by Gordon W. Gahan

☐ BOOKS FOR YOUNG EXPLORERS
NATIONAL GEOGRAPHIC SOCIETY

COPYRIGHT © 1975 NATIONAL GEOGRAPHIC SOCIETY   LIBRARY OF CONGRESS CATALOG NUMBER 75-6068   INTERNATIONAL STANDARD BOOK NUMBER 0-87044-169-8

Harley and Joan run deeper and deeper into the forest.
The dry leaves crackle under their feet.

When they stop, the forest seems very quiet, as if nothing lives there.
Do you think that is true? Let's follow Harley and Joan and find out.

When the children look up, the treetops are like a roof over their heads.
The leafy branches keep out some of the sunlight,
and the forest is shady and cool.
The trees make fine homes for many animals of the forest.
The gray squirrel sits on a branch crunching on a nut.
It shakes its tail and chatters as the children walk by.

SOUTHERN FLYING SQUIRREL

GRAY SQUIRREL

The flying squirrel leaps
from a branch high in a tree.
Flaps of skin on each side
spread out like wings.
Then the squirrel glides
down to another tree.

5

The opossum family sleeps all day inside a hollow tree.
The mother comes out at night to hunt for food.
Her babies ride along. They hold onto the fur on her back.

Raccoons look as if
they are wearing masks.
They sleep during the day
in their den high in a tree.
Raccoons dunk their food,
whenever they can find water.

A woodpecker has just fed an insect
to one of its chicks. Like all baby birds,
the young woodpeckers are very hungry.
Woodpeckers peck at
the bark of trees with sharp beaks.
They make holes in trees for nests
and eat insects that live under the bark.

7

GREAT HORNED OWL NESTLINGS

These baby owls live
at the top of a dead tree.
Their parents are good hunters.
Owls swoop down
and find little rabbits or mice
even in the dark.

The two cedar waxwings,
like most birds, live in trees.
But they come to the ground
to splash in puddles
for their baths.
The bobwhite lives on the ground
and makes its nest there.
It usually walks
from place to place.
But it also can fly very fast.

9

Joan and Harley have caught a turtle.
It is one of the slowest animals
in the forest. Could you catch a turtle?
When Harley and Joan pick it up,
the turtle pulls its head, legs, and tail
back into its shell.
It waits for them to go away.

Two deer have come
to a grassy spot in the forest.
They nibble grass still wet with dew.
As they eat, they stop and look around.
They sniff the air and listen.
If enemies are near,
they run away very fast.
Later they curl up
and rest for most of the day.

BOX TURTLE

WHITE-TAILED DEER

A tiny mouse
with big whiskers
tickles the back of
Joan's hand.

A green flower
called jack-in-the-pulpit
grows in the shade.
Do you see the pulpit?

COTTON MOUSE

BEAVER

The beaver is very busy.
With sharp teeth, it cuts down young trees.
It uses the trees to build a dam across a stream.
The dam makes a pond where the beaver can build its house.

Young rabbits feed and play at night.
They spend the day keeping very quiet.
They hold still so their enemies won't see them.
Just their little noses twitch.

JACK-IN-THE-PULPIT

EASTERN COTTONTAIL RABBIT

A bobcat has climbed onto a big rock.
It drinks from a puddle of water there.
The bobcat has sharp claws and teeth.
It hunts mostly at night.
It looks for small animals like rabbits and chipmunks.
If it sees a chipmunk, it very quietly creeps close to it.
Then suddenly the bobcat pounces on the chipmunk.
Sometimes the little chipmunk is lucky and can run away.

GREEN ANOLE

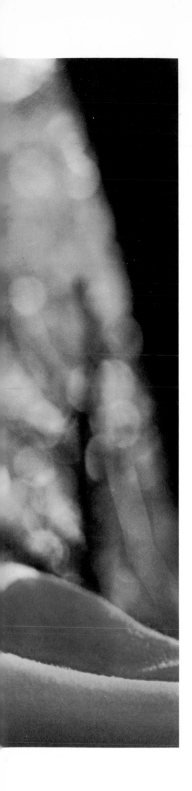

CRICKET FROG

GREEN TREE FROG

A brown lizard with a long tail crawls on Harley's hand.
The lizard can also turn green. When it is on a leaf, it is hard to see.
Joan holds a tiny cricket frog in her fingers.
She looks at it through a magnifying glass.
Harley looks carefully and finds a frog on a leaf.
If you were small and green, would you try to hide on a plant?

The forest is full of insects.
They live everywhere:
in trees, on the ground,
in streams.
A brown walkingstick
looks like a twig.
So it is hard to see.

The praying mantis
catches other insects
with its long front legs.

A dragonfly has just wiggled
out of its skin.
As an insect grows,
its skin becomes too tight.
Then the skin splits.
New skin is underneath.

Butterflies fly
through the forest.
They bring color,
like spots of sunshine.

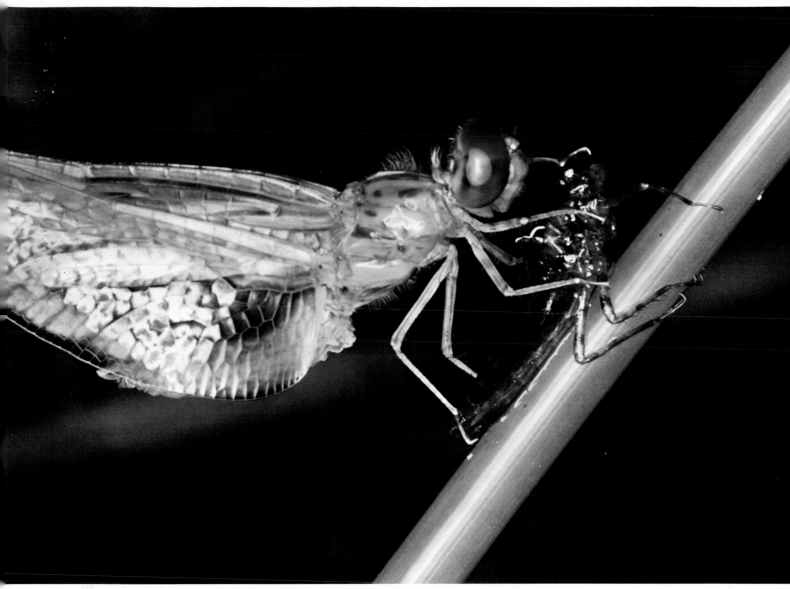

NEWLY-EMERGED ADULT DRAGONFLY

BUCKEYE BUTTERFLY

LITTLE METALMARK BUTTERFLY

A little stream with muddy banks runs through the forest.
Some animals come to the stream for a drink.
Others drink dew or raindrops.
These turtles are called cooters. They live in the stream.
They like to crawl out on a log
and warm themselves in the sun.

COOTERS

LARVA OF RUSTY MUD SALAMANDER

Harley and Joan carefully cross the stream on a log.
The children carry plastic boxes for collecting insects and plants.
The salamander in Joan's hand is so slippery it is hard to hold.
Can you see the little gills that stick out behind its head?
The young salamander has gills for breathing in water.
When it is grown, it can breathe in the air. Then it lives on land.

A snake! Joan has found a scarlet king snake on the forest floor.
She knows it is not poisonous. So she picks it up.
Its skin feels smooth and dry. The snake wiggles and tries to get away.
The king snake looks like a poisonous snake, called the coral snake.
Never pick up any snake, unless an adult tells you it is not poisonous!
Snakes shed their skins as insects do.
Joan and Harley find a piece of skin a snake has left behind.
Later, Joan stops and feels the rough bark of a pine tree.
When the bark is rough, a corn snake can climb a tree without slipping.

A dead log in the forest is like an apartment house.
Creatures of all kinds move in.
Some live under it. Some live in it.
Some dig tunnels in the ground below it.
The children find two earthworms and a slug.
Some eggs look like little balls of glass.
Slugs and snails lay eggs like these.
A shiny black beetle crawls on Harley's knee.
Next to it is a millipede with many legs.
It pulls in its legs and curls up like a wheel.
The gray beetle larva will soon turn into an adult.
The land snail lives in its shell.
Inside, it looks like a slug.
After many years the log will be gone.
The plants and animals that feed on the log
help to change it into soil.

LEAF LICHEN AND BEARD LICHEN

Harley sits on a log and looks at green plants from the swamp nearby.
A swamp is a place where the land is always wet and muddy.
The little twig on the ground has two plants growing on it.
They are lichens. Lichens don't need soil. They even grow on rocks.
There are some plants that don't need sunlight.
These two fungus plants live on sick or dead trees.
The white Indian pipe lives on dead leaves.

LEATHERY GILL FUNGUS

INDIAN PIPE

VARIEGATED
SHELL FUNGUS

27

The children find some leafy ferns growing in shady parts of the forest.
Poison ivy can grow in shady spots too.
The children are careful not to touch it.
The oil in the plant can give them a very bad rash and blisters.
Trees need sunlight. Many young trees won't get enough light to live.
Fire, insects, and beavers will kill others.
But the trees that remain will have room to grow.

Joan and Harley
dig up a young tree.
They carry it
to a sunny spot.
They replant it
so it will have
room to grow.

PINE SEEDLING

POISON IVY

WILD AZALEA

Time to go home.
The day has ended.
The shadows grow longer.
Harley's father carries the children
through the water of the swamp.
They have seen beauty and wonder
—in a spider web, in a wild flower.
They have learned
that there are many things
to see and do in a forest.
A forest is a busy place.
It is filled with life.
Something is happening all the time.

Published by The National Geographic Society
Melvin M. Payne, *President;* Melville Bell Grosvenor, *Editor-in-Chief;* Gilbert M. Grosvenor, *Editor*

Prepared by
The Special Publications Division
Robert L. Breeden, *Editor*
Donald J. Crump, *Associate Editor*
Philip B. Silcott, *Senior Editor*
Cynthia Russ Ramsay, *Managing Editor*
Elizabeth W. Fisher, *Research*

Illustrations
David R. Bridge, *Picture Editor*

Design and Art Direction
Joseph A. Taney, *Staff Art Director*
Josephine B. Bolt, *Associate Art Director*
Ursula Perrin, *Assistant Art Director*

Production and Printing
Robert W. Messer, *Production Manager*
George V. White, *Assistant Production Manager*
Raja D. Murshed, June L. Graham, *Production Assistants*
John R. Metcalfe, *Engraving and Printing*
Mary G. Burns, Jane H. Buxton, Stephanie S. Cooke, Suzanne J. Jacobson,
Marilyn L. Wilbur, *Staff Assistants*

Consultants
Dr. Glenn O. Blough, Peter L. Munroe, *Educational Consultants*
Edith K. Chasnov, *Reading Specialist*
Tall Timbers Research Station and Smithsonian Institution, Washington, D. C., *Scientific Consultants*

Illustrations Credits

All photographs by Gordon W. Gahan, *National Geographic photographic staff except:* L. L. Rue
III, *(12 bottom), Bruce Coleman Inc. (6);* Thase Daniel, *Bruce Coleman Inc. (7 left);* Fred J. Alsop
III, *Bruce Coleman Inc. (7 right);* E. R. Degginger, *Bruce Coleman Inc. (13 bottom, 18 left, 19
bottom left);* David R. Bridge, *National Geographic staff (13 top, 27 right);* Trudy Unverhau,
Animals Animals (14 top); Mark Stouffer *(14-15);* Lynn M. Stone *(16 bottom); Bruce Coleman Inc.
(18 right);* David Hughes, *Bruce Coleman Inc. (19 top);* John Shaw, *Bruce Coleman Inc. (19
bottom right);* James P. Jackson *(25 bottom center, 32);* Dick Durrance II, *National Geographic
photographic staff (30 top).*

Endpaper drawings by Tony Chen

One day this little acorn may grow
into a tall oak tree.

Some animals in the Day in the Woods *hunt for food in the evening or at night.*